Good Thoughts

Good Words   *Good Deeds*

THE MESSIAH: SAOSHYANT

Who were the Magi in the Gospel of Matthew searching for their messiah?

BY: BAHRAM SPITAMA

Table of Contents

About The Author iii
Acknowledgement vii
Glossary ix

Introduction: The concept of a Savior 1
CHAPTER 1: The Messiah in ancient Persia 9
Ancient Persian Savior: Mithra 9
The "Miraculous Birth" and Virgin Mother 10
Yalda Celebration 11
Mithra's influence in Roman's empire 12
Zarathustra: The Savior - Saoshyant 13
The Magi 16

CHAPTER 2: Influence of Zoroastrianism on Judaism 22
King Cyrus: Jewish messiah 22
Savior or Messiah 28
Messiah in Judaism 28
Messiah in Zoroastrianism 30

CHAPTER 3: Esoteric vs. Exoteric knowledge 33

CONCLUSION 46

ABOUT THE AUTHOR

BAHRAM MOTERASSED (Spitama)[1] has been a psychotherapist for thirty years, incorporating Eastern spirituality into his practice. He has a BA in psychology and a master's degree in marriage and family therapy. He has studied and practiced Sufism, Buddhism, Yoga, Mazdaism, Christianity, Kabbalah, and sweat lodges. He has also practiced and taught meditation courses for more than thirty years. Bahram is the author of Born to Fly, You Are Beyond Who You Are, Good Thoughts, Good Words, Good Deeds, and Your Immortal Spirit: From Death to Deathlessness.

www.zarathustra.ca

---

[1] Spitama is chosen here because of the author's immense love and respect for the wisdom of Zarathustra Spitama.

Acknowledgement

I would like to dedicate this book to Dr. Henry Maurice Nicoll (19 July 1884 – 30 August 1953). He was a Scottish neurologist and psychiatrist who contributed to the esoteric teaching of the four Gospels and his psychological interpretation of the meanings and parables in the New Testament. All sacred and ancient teachings contain an outer and an inner meaning, whether taken literally or metaphorically. Nicoll's interpretation of the teachings of Christ went beyond their ordinary meanings. He offered an esoteric and psychological understanding of the stories and parables from the Gospels.

Since wisdom and the higher understanding of our purpose on Earth is difficult to explain scientifically and literally, the ancient teachings used metaphors, stories, and parables to convey their messages. A parable serves as a medium to connect our higher being with our lower one. The purpose of sacred teachings is like seeds that need to fall into the soil of our consciousness to grow and yield fruits of deeper meaning. Each sacred word is concealed within an inner and esoteric meaning. Each parable is pregnant with many potentials and understanding, needing to unveil itself from its earthly understanding to its "Heavenly" meanings. I am grateful to Maurice Nicoll for his psychological and esoteric interpretation of Christ's sacred teachings. Peace be with his soul.

This book is also dedicated to French linguistic scholar Abraham Anqetil-Duperron (1731–1805), who translated the Gathas (Zarathustra Sublime Songs). For the first time after thousands of years, we now clearly understand Zarathustra's wisdom.

It needs to be pointed out that this book is based on the esoteric teachings of Zarathustra, carried by the Magi after his death. The Magi established the path of Mazda-Yasna, meaning "the followers of wisdom." This book explores the inner meaning of Zarathustra's teachings from the Mazda-Yasna perspective rather than from the religious practices of Zoroastrianism.

Glossary

Ahriman	Wicked thought/spirit/energy/anger, *Angra Mainyu* in the *Gathas,* Satan in English
Ahura Mazda	The Sublime Wisdom, the essence, the Supreme Consciousness, God in English both masculine and feminine
	Ahura: masculine, consciousness, light
	Mazda: feminine, wisdom, life
Amesha Spenta	Immortal Bounteous, seven attributes of Ahura Mazda
Angra Mainyu	The spirit of ignorance, unconsciousness, wickedness, anger in English, *Ahriman,* Satan in English
Asha/Artha	Harmony, balance, *Artha,* art in English, harmony
Frashokereti	"Making wonderful/excellent." It is a notion of a final restoration of the universe to its original perfect creation
Fravashi	Authentic self, true self/spirit, our essence, "I," angel, guardian angel in English, "Holy Souls"

Gathas	Songs, the Sublime Songs of Zarathustra composed by himself about five thousand years ago, the only surviving Indo-European language
Mainyu	Mind in English, spirit, energy, way of thinking
Soashyant	Guide, Savior, Messiah in Zarathustra's concept
Spenta	Sacred, holy, progressive
Spenta Mainyu	Sacred wisdom, good mind, progressive mentality, Holy Spirit in English
Spitama	Zarathustra, also known as meaning "pure"
Zarathustra	Zarathustra was an enlightened person who lived about five thousand years ago in Persia (Iran), the founder of the Zoroastrian religion and Mazdaism (seeker of wisdom)

INTRODUCTION

The concept of a Savior

One day, I was driving on a country road to visit someone. It was minus 35 in a cold winter month in Canada with lots of snow on the road. Suddenly, my car slipped into the ditch and could not get out. Not many cars were passing by, and there was no signal reception to call for help. The next town was very far away, and I could not walk on the road to get there due to the extreme cold. I tried first to get out, but the car was getting deeper into the snow and became more stuck as I was trying harder. Finally, I gave up and sat in the car. The only thing that I could do was to sit and wait. I surrendered myself to whatever will be, will be.

It was getting darker, and I was worried about running out of gas if I kept the engine going to be warm. After some time that felt like an eternity, I saw a car approaching me. I got out to inform the driver about my condition. It was a pickup truck, and the person stopped for me. He was a farmer. He had a cable, and his truck was equipped to pull my car out of the ditch. After I got out, I told him that "You are my savior. You saved me."

This short story is about one of the people who rescued me in my life. I am 62 years old and I have had many other times when I felt really hopeless. Just when I thought there was no way out, something or someone came to help me. We can think of these moments as either accidental, coincidence, Karma, or perhaps there was an invisible force looking out for me. I am not the only one who has experienced these kinds of events. We all have times when something or someone shows up just in time to rescue us when we need it in times of despair. Can you remember and be thankful for something similar happening in your life?

Once, a man lost everything he owned and didn't have a place to live anymore. He was very embarrassed to face his family and friends. He thought about ending his life. Just then, a mystic came by. The mystic asked him what was wrong. The man shared that he had lost everything and didn't see much reason to live. The mystic told him that he was already a wealthy man, and he could prove it. If he had followed the mystic that night, he would have been wealthy again the next day. The mystic promised him that If he didn't get his wealth back, he could choose to end his life the next day. The man agreed and followed the mystic.

They walked in silence together until they arrived at someone's house. The mystic knocked on the door, and a man who was blind opened it. The mystic told the man he knew he would give anything to be able to see. He asked how much he was willing to pay in order to have the eyes of the mystic's companion. The blind man was ready to give all he had, which was over $200,000. The mystic looked at his companion and asked him if he was willing to accept the offer for his eyes. The man said, "No."

They walked together again until they reached a house where a disabled man in a wheelchair opened the door. The mystic asked him how much he would pay to walk again. The man said, "I don't have a lot of money, but my family does. I would borrow $300,000 if I could walk again." The mystic turned to his companion once more. He was being offered a large amount of money to give up his legs. The mystic asked if he would accept. The man said, "No."

Then, they came to a home where a family had lost their son in a war. They were heartbroken and in deep sorrow. The mystic asked them how much they would give to have their son back alive. They said, with tears in their eyes, that they would give away everything in order to have their son alive again. The mystic turned to his fellow companion and asked whether he would accept their offer, but he needed to sacrifice his son. The man said, "No." He asked the mystic to stop the test. He now understood how fortunate and wealthy he truly was. He thanked the mystic and went back to his family and worked hard to regain his wealth. The mystic was indeed the man's savior.

Human beings are social animals. We are not meant to be alone and live in isolation alone without helping one another. We meant to be together and help each other at the time of need. If we look around, there are saviors everywhere. When the house is on fire, the firefighters come to save us and our homes at such a critical time. When we are injured or have a heart attack, the doctors and nurses rush to save us from our urgent circumstances. When we have a plumbing issue and are out of running water, a plumber is our savior and rescuer. When we look deep into our existence, we realize at some point in our lives either we rushed to save someone in their desperate time, or we have been saved by many people throughout our lifespan.

We are meant to help each other and to rescue one another as human beings. This is an important aspect of humanity.

> *Human beings are members of a whole*
> *In creation of one essence and soul*
> *If one member is afflicted with pain*
> *Other members uneasy will remain*
> *If you have no sympathy for human pain*
> *The name of human you cannot retain.*
>
> Persian mystic & poet - Saadi

In addition to individual experiences, many nations, cities, towns, and ethnic groups have their heroes who have made immense sacrifices to protect and uplift their people during critical moments in history. For instance, Martin Luther King was an important figure in the American civil rights movement. He dedicated his life to fighting against racial discrimination and segregation. His dedication and ultimate sacrifice that he made continue to inspire people worldwide. Nelson Mandela was a brave leader in South Africa. He experienced years of imprisonment to combat apartheid and promote freedom and equality in his nation. His tireless efforts for justice influenced not only his nation but also became a symbol of hope for oppressed people everywhere.

Joan of Arc was a brave young woman who led her people during a critical time in France. Her courage and determination reunited her people and influenced their history. Others like Socrates, Pythagoras, and Galileo challenged established beliefs and dogma to advance human knowledge and understanding. They stood firm to pursue truth, eventhough they were faced persecution or torture. King Cyrus, a Persian leader who freed Jews from their captivities in Babylon. He is known as a messiah in Judaism and is highly respected for diversity and religious freedom. He became an extraordinary example of human rights and diverse religious practices for his time and then after.

In addition, we also have fictional saviors and heroes such as Superman, Batman, and Spiderman. They represent ideals of goodness, justice, and selflessness. These characters, as our superheroes, inspire us by showing individuals who can protect humanity from dark forces with their incredible strengths and readiness to sacrifice for our well-being. Even as imaginary figures, they offer us comfort and a sense of security. They serve as powerful role models as examples of willingness and compassion to face danger through their selfless and sacrificial nature. They remind us that anyone can be a hero by doing good things for others.

The idea of a savior is a concept that can be found in various religions and belief systems worldwide throughout history as well. It is a belief that a special individual who has the divine power to rescue or save humanity in times of despair would come. The difference between these individuals and the above examples is that they are meant to rescue human souls and spirits for a higher good and purpose. They often called themselves healers, such as Yeshua (Jesus in Greek).[2] They did not come to heal or cure our physical bodies, but to heal our souls in times of ignorance, violence, corruption, and greed. In other faiths, there are similar figures like Buddha. He was

---

[2] In this book, the name Yeshua is used instead of Jesus. It's important to note that Jesus's real name in Hebrew was Yeshua, which is translated to Joshua in English. The name Jesus was assigned by the Greeks many years after his crucifixion. However, the historically accurate name for him is Yeshua.

an enlightened person who came to guide humanity and to liberate us from the cycle of suffering and rebirth (Samsara).

Zarathustra who lived about 5000 years ago in Persia (modern day Iran)[3] was also a savior. For the first time, he brought the concept of a savior as a messiah (Saoshyant). He came as a savior or Saoshyant to wake up humanity from the spirit of unconsciousness and ignorance. Saoshyant means at its root "the one who brings benefit to humankind" to lead righteousness over wickedness. He also declared that after him there will be other messiahs or Saoshyants coming to finish his teaching and to lead humanity toward light and salvation from deceptions and to make the Earth like paradise. Saoshyant is considered a future savior or messianic figure to lead humanity toward the wisdom of the Supreme Being (Ahura Mazda). He informed us in the Gathas (his Sublime Songs) that

> *O Mazda Ahura, the path that You have shown me is the path of good thoughts and the teachings and guidance of the **Soshyants** (Saviors).*[4]

The concept of a savior goes back centuries before the time of Zarathustra. For instance, in Egyptian mythology, there is a savior figure known as Horus. He is an ancient Egyptian deity, often depicted as a falcon-headed man or as a falcon. He was God of sky and was known as "The Messiah" by the ancient Egyptians. Before Zarathustra, Mithra was known by Indo-Iranians. Mithra was god of the rising sun. He was a savior figure who freed humanity from darkness and deception by bringing light and order to Earth.

---

[3] The name officially changed from Persia to Iran in 1935.

[4] Yasna 34.13

In this book, the idea of the messiah (Saoshyant) from ancient Persian times and the teachings of Zarathustra will be explored. The Magi, who were followers of Zarathustra, anticipated the arrival of their Saoshyant as prophesied by Zarathustra around the time of Yeshua's (Jesus) birth. We've all heard of the Magi in the Bible, those wise men from the East who followed a shining star to honor the birth of Yeshua. But who were they? What did they believe? And why did they go on such a long journey? It's interesting how they seem to fade from historical records. Also, what was so important about following that special star?

This book aims to give readers insights into the story of the Magi in the Gospel of Matthew and their role from a Persian spiritual perspective (Mazdayasna based on Zarathiustra's teachings). It is not meant to be historical or academic literature.

CHAPTER 1

The Messiah in ancient Persia

Ancient Persian Savior: Mithra

Traditionally, ancient Persian worshiped a multitude of gods. They had gods (e.g., Mithra) and goddesses (e.g., Anahita). Mithra was the god of the rising sun. He was the protector of people and came to bring justice and order on Earth. It was believed by Persians that Mithra took on human form while staying divine and was sent to Earth to guide humanity to the true path. The name Mithra comes from the Indo-European root "mihr," which means both "friend" and "contract."[5]

The Sun was viewed not only to illuminate Earth but he was also considered as a 'Creator,' 'Ruler,' 'Preserver,' and 'Savior' of the world.[6] The Sun (Mithra) was considered as a Savior since there would not be any life on Earth without its light and warmth. Mithra became the savior of human beings because he brought light and defeated darkness. He was perceived as the preserver and protector of truth and justice because he revealed

---
[5] Goodswen, Oliver. *Mithra the Forgotten Mystery God.* Trell Book Publishers, 2016.
[6] Titcomb, Sarah. *Aryan Sun-Myths.* Jazzybee Verlag, 2017.

everything to us out of the darkness and our ignorance. Sunday (Sun-Day) was a special day dedicated to him to honor his divine's presence. There was an exchange, while Mithra was a Creator and a Savior of people, humans were expected to honor and to worship him in return. It was believed that Mithra was born from an immaculate birth from a virgin mother named Anahita.

The "Miraculous Birth" and Virgin Mother

The concept of a Virgin-Born Savior was well-known in ancient Persia for centuries. The idea of the virgin mother in Persian culture comes from the Goddess Anahita. She is the ancient Persian goddess of fertility, water, health and healing, and wisdom.[7] She symbolizes cleanliness and purity. She is often presented as water, Venus, or moon.

Anahita is the personification of Venus and the moon goddess, governing tides and fertility. As the supreme star deity of ancient Persia, she guided and protected travelers. Connected to the sun god Mithras, her influence extended beyond the night sky. As the 'Shining One,' she is also a war goddess, riding through the skies in a chariot drawn by four horses: Wind, Rain, Cloud, and Hail.

Across various ancient cultures, water and wisdom are often linked. In Persian culture, Anahita embodies wisdom and femininity. She's called a "Virgin" metaphorically, symbolizing purity and absence of falsehood or ignorance rather than literal virginity. Her name in the Zoroastrian Avesta, Aredvi Sura Anahita, signifies moistness, strength, and purity. In the Avesta,

---

7 Mark, Joshua J. "Anahita." *World History Encyclopedia*, 2020.

THE MESSIAH: SAOSHYANT

she's described as purifying seeds, ensuring safe childbirth, and providing adequate and quality milk for nursing.[8]

She's known as the "Mother-Goddess" and the "Mother of all beings." She's also the mother of Mithra, who represents the sun and light and is said to be born without a father. Mithra is a Persian god who watches over the sunrise, agreements, friendships, and teamwork. He also keeps the seasons balanced and gives kings blessings to rule. Warriors also see him as a protector and ask for his help before battles, which is why he's called a war god.[9]

Yalda Celebration

For over 7000 years in Persia, Mithra's birthday was celebrated on Dec 22. "Yalda" means "birth" and marks both Mithra's birth and the Winter Solstice. Yalda is still celebrated in Iran today and is linked with the birth of the Savior, Mithra, symbolizing the victory of light over darkness. This celebration occurs around December 21, the longest night of the year, signaling the start of longer days as the sun (Mithra, the Savior) is "born" again. It signifies the sun's return and the lengthening of days.

Traditionally, family and friends spend time together at the Yalda night (Shab-e Yalda شب یلدا) and stay awake until sunrise. During this celebration, families and friends enjoy food, drinks, and poetry readings. In ancient Persia, Yalda was celebrated with an evergreen tree, similar to the Christmas tree, often a pine or spruce. The evergreen tree symbolizes human resilience

---

[8] Darmesteter, James, translator. "Avesta: Khorda Avesta. ABAN YASHT ('Hymn to the Waters') 5:2." *Sacred Books of the East, American Edition, 1898.*

[9] Mark, Joshua J. "Mithra." *World History Encyclopedia, 2020.*

and endurance during the harsh winter (associated with Ahriman, the wicked spirit).

Mithra's influence in Roman's empire

Eventually, the worship of Mithra spread from Persia to Asia Minor and later came to Egyptian tradition about 200 BC and Roman culture. The worship of Mithra reached Rome later on, but its beliefs and rituals remained largely consistent. The Persian Mysteries spread across the Roman Empire due to the movement of soldiers and trade. Sites dedicated to Mithras were discovered along the borders of Roman expansion, including Britain, Germany, Romania, Spain, North Africa, Armenia, and within the Empire itself, such as in Italy, Gaul, Bulgaria, Asia Minor (Turkey), Syria, Palestine, and Rome.[10]

Mithra, the Sun God, transitioned from Persian to Roman culture. Despite conflicts between Romans and Persians, Romans embraced the pre-Zoroastrian cult of Mithra. Interestingly, Romans celebrated Mithras' birthday on Dec 25, a date more closely associated with the ancient Egyptian god Horus than with Persian traditions. Horus was born on December 25th from a virgin mother and was a savior similar to Mithra as well.

In "Mithras, the Secret God,"[11] Vermaseren describes a ritual among Roman Mithraic worshippers involving the slaying of a bull, consuming its flesh, and drinking its blood for soul salvation. However, Zarathustra's teachings challenged

---

[10] Goodswen, Oliver. *Mithra the Forgotten Mystery God*. Trell Book Publishers, 2016.

[11] Vermaseren, M. *Mithras, the Secret God*. Barnes & Noble, 1963, p. 103.

ancient Persian polytheism about 5000 years ago, introducing a monastic concept and forbidding animal sacrifices in Mithraic temples. Bull-slaying tradition persisted in Roman culture until they adopted Christianity as the state religion in the 4th century AD.

Zarathustra: The Savior - Saoshyant

It's hard to know an exact date for Zarathustra's life because we have very little information about it. The best way to estimate when he lived comes from studying the language used in the hymns he wrote, known as the Gathas (songs). Most experts believe that he lived roughly 5000 to 7000 years ago. The Gathas is a collection of hymns and is one of the oldest languages that has survived to our time. When you listen to the songs of the Gathas, one has a glimpse of how Indo-Europeans used to speak. Some of the words are similar to English. For example, 'Angra' means anger, 'Mainyu' means mind, and 'Asha' (or 'Artha', meaning harmony and balance) means art.

Zarathustra was the title given to him later after his enlightenment. **Zar**atha means gold (Zar in Persian means gold) and Ushtra means Light or star, shining (Astra, هراتس in Persian). He was known before as Spitama (Pure). Zarathustra means, "The Shining Star," or "The one who possesses the Golden Light". The word "enlightenment" was later used as a spiritual term after his name. It is the root of the word astrology, meaning to study the influences of the stars and planets on human affairs and circumstances.

Ancient Persians worshiped a different god for rain, prosperity, health, sunshine, earthquakes or floods. He challenged the old tradition of the Indo-European religions that was practiced before him and created an awareness and movement that eventually became the dominant religion in Persia. Zarathushtra was a mage of the original Indo-European religion (Mithraism), which was practiced nearly 5,000 years ago. He universalized aspects of Indo-European concepts into a sophisticated and abstract ideology.

Zarathustra's teachings were revolutionary for his era, a time dominated by violence, slavery, and oppression. He was deeply troubled by what he witnessed: a degradation of the human spirit, cruelty to animals, and environmental destruction. He challenged the prevailing corruption and injustices not through force or violence, but by seeking to shift minds through reason, wisdom, and awareness. Zarathustra envisioned a society and world where individuals were empowered to think independently and choose their own destinies instead of blindly following. He opposed conformity and urged people to seek wisdom and knowledge from enlightened individuals. He believed in the innate goodness of each person and encouraged them to cultivate goodness in their thoughts, words, and actions.

His teachings also established the religion of Zoroastrianism and the esoteric school of Mazdaism. It became the dominant religion of the Persian Empires: The Achaemenid (c. 550–330 BCE), Parthians (c. 247 BCE–224 CE), and Sasanian (224–651 CE). It remained the state religion of the Persian Empire until about the seventh century CE, when Muslims conquered Persia. Due to several invasions by Greeks, Arabs, and Mongols in Persia, many of the wisdom teachings and esoteric schools were destroyed. Due to the evolution of the Persian language over time, Zarathustra's hymns (the Gathas) were not understood until the eighteenth century CE when Anquetil-Duperron, a French linguistic scholar, translated them into French.

Zarathustra referred to The Messiah as Soshyants, meaning "the one who brings benefit" to humanity. In The Gathas, he mentioned that other spiritual guides (Soshyant-Messiah) would come after him in the future to further his mission and liberate humanity from corruption and deception, leading to universal salvation. He attributed several of his sacred hymns to a future figure called Saoshyant, believing that anointed individuals appointed by Ahura Mazda (The Supreme Being) would guide people towards a conscientious and compassionate life on Earth.

Indeed, the Soshyantsand the saviors of the world will be those who, by following good thoughts, fulfill their duty.[12]

O Mazda, show me the true path of good thoughts. Also, inform Soshyant (the savior) of the reward for his work.[13]

According to Zarathustra, several Saoshyants would be born throughout history and across different ethnicities to spread the message of universal salvation among humanity. For many centuries after Zarathustra's death, his followers were known as Magi or Mobed (in modern Persian). Surviving Zoroastrian texts indicate that ancient Zoroastrians and Magi used astrology to measure historical and calendrical time and events. The Magi developed astrological calendars to measure

---

[12] Yasna 48-12

[13] Yasna 48-9

time, predict seasons, and anticipate climate changes.[14] During the Parthian period prior to the birth of Yeshua (Jesus), the Magi (Zoroastrian priests) were anticipating the arrival of their messiah, as promised by their prophet Zarathustra.

The Magi

After Jesus was born in Bethlehem in Judea, during the time of King Herod, Magi from the east came to Jerusalem 2 and asked, "Where is the one who has been born king of the Jews? We saw his star when it rose and have come to worship him."[15]

We have all heard, no doubt, of the story of the Magi in the Bible, traveling from the East, following a shining star to welcome the birth of Yeshua. What made them believe that this new-born child was really the Messiah (the Anointed One, the Savior), the one they had been waiting for? Why did they bring three gifts? Sadly, the Western world knows little of these Magi. They were, in fact, Persian Magi or Zoroastrian priests who followed the star.

Although Matthew never mentioned in his Gospel the number of Magi visiting Bethlehem, three Magi did not enter into the Christian tradition until later since they offered three gifts to Yeshua (Jesus). Except for Matthew, the story of the Magi was not found in other Gospels of The New Testament. The Magi were those who had the wisdom of Zarathustra's teachings and were knowledgeable of the birth of the Messiah coming at the time of Yeshua's birth. They did not just follow a shining

---

[14] Flowers, Stephen E., Ph.D. *Original Magic: The Rituals and Initiations of the Persian Magi.* Inner Traditions, 2017.

[15] Matthew 2:1-3 NIV

star out of curiosity or a coincidence, they had great knowledge about a Messiah's birth and the timing of it. They knew exactly who to seek and where to go. They were not kings, but advisors of kings in Persian empires.

The New World Encyclopedia[16] states that the word Magi refers to ancient Zoroastrian astrologer-priests who were living in the Persian Empire. The term "Magi" originates from the Greek word "magos" (μαγος pl. μαγοι), which was borrowed from Old Persian "maguš." In Greek, "maguš" comes from the Indo-Iranian root "magh," meaning "powerful, rich." The modern Persian term "Mobed" (referring to Zoroastrian priests) comes from the Old Persian compound "magu-pati," meaning "lord priest." Zoroastrian priests, known as "magha" or "maga," were referred to by the Greeks as the "Magi" (singular: magus).

To find the original meaning of "Magi," scholars look to ancient Iran and the teachings of Zarathustra. He referred to his first group of followers, who sought wisdom through his teachings, as the "Assembly of Magi." These individuals were followers of Mazdaism and Zarathustra. They reached a high level of awareness and were respected as wise leaders who shared Zarathustra's teachings with others. As Zoroastrian high priests, they focused on self-improvement and helping others, following their prophet's guidance for personal and collective growth.

Metaphorically, the Magi were called kings because they attained the highest level of consciousness in the Crown chakra, which is associated with enlightenment, life's purpose,

---

[16] *"Magi." New World Encyclopedia*
https://www.newworldencyclopedia.org/entry/Magi

and spirituality. Similarly, Yeshua also referred to himself as a "King" due to his early increase in wisdom and stature. The Bible states, "And Jesus grew in wisdom and stature, and in favour with God and man."[17] This led to confusion among his people and the Romans, who questioned how a mere Rabbi could claim to be the "King of the Jews." Roman soldiers even mocked him before his crucifixion by placing a crown made of thorn bushes on his head.

One of Plato's disciples, Hermodorus, called Zoroaster a Persian and the first Magi.[18] The first fellowship of believers who gathered around Zarathustra seeking wisdom were called the "Assembly of Magi". Similarly Christian mythology has Yeshua choosing twelve disciples, so Zoroaster had his inner circle. The Roman orator Cicero (106-43 BC) also stated, "Indeed, no one can become king of the Persians until he has learned the theory and the practice of the Magi."[19]

The Magi were present alongside King Cyrus from his earliest campaigns, including the capture of Babylon. They established the school of Mazdaism shortly after and later influenced Greek philosophy, as seen with Pythagoras during his time among the Magi.

> While in Egypt, Pythagoras was taken captive by the soldiers of Cambyses [the Persian king] and brought to Babylon. He was later released under some mysterious circumstances. He took this opportunity to make his own research in the god science in Babylon.

---

[17] Luke 2:52 NIV

[18] Eduljee, K. E. "Zoroastrian Heritage: Greek Perceptions of Zoroaster, Zoroastrianism & the Magi." April 25, 2011.

[19] Cicero. *On Divination Book I. De Divinatione.* Loeb Classical Library, 1923.

> *He met the spiritual heads of the magi and learned the science of numbers, arithmetic, the Chaldean branch of astronomy and astrology, as well as music. He was accepted as a Master of these branches of wisdom.*[20]

> *In Babylon he [Pythagoras] was able to thoroughly study the knowledge in the possession of the magi, the heirs of Zoroaster.*[21]

The Magi were highly skilled in various disciplines such as astrology, cosmology, psychology, meditation, herbology, alchemy, and possessed remarkable healing abilities. Their school was focused on esoteric teachings and held great spiritual mysteries, which were closely guarded and only revealed to a select few who were prepared to seek the truth. The Persian mystic poet Hafiz, from the 14th century, praised the wisdom of the Magi who gathered in Zarathustra's inner circle during his time, referring to them as "The Divine light."[22]

The Magi aimed to lead people towards self-transformation and a higher state of being. They believed that humanity's main purpose was to attain this elevated consciousness, leading to a life of balance, harmony, and inner happiness while also living gently on Earth. As Zoroastrian high priests, the Magi possessed extensive knowledge about the identity and birth of their awaited Messiah (Saoshyant or savior, as promised by Zarathustra in the Gathas). They recognized and understood Yeshua's birth on a deeper spiritual level than the people in

---

[20] Schuré, Édouard. The Wisdom of Pythagoras. Createspace Independent Publishing Platform, 2015.

[21] Schuré, Édouard. Pythagoras and the Delphic Mysteries. Cosimo Classics, 2007.

[22] Hafiz, Ghazal 357.

Judea. They were among the first to celebrate the birth of Yeshua (Jesus), recognizing him as their awaited Saoshyant (Messiah).

Judea had been part of the Persian Empire before coming under Roman rule during Yeshua's time. Judea was caught in a proxy war between the Roman and Parthian Empires during this period. The Parthian Empire, a significant political and cultural force from 247 BC to 224 AD, held sway over Asian territories, with its origins in northeastern Iran. Zoroastrianism, the major religion of the Persian Empires for centuries, was the state religion for over a millennium until the Muslim invasion in the 7th century (633-654 AD).

Venus, known as the "light-bringer," has two distinct phases a :morning star and an evening star. It is the brightest natural object in Earth's sky, visible even in daylight. In Zoroastrian mythology, the Goddess Anahita (associated with Venus) is symbolically pregnant with the sun's light (representing God, Ahura Mazda), and she gives birth to the sun in the morning (symbolized by Mithra). The star of Bethlehem in the Gospel of Matthew, which the Magi followed, is believed by some to represent Venus, symbolizing the virgin mother (Anahita) about to give birth to the new star (representing the Saoshyant or Messiah, symbolized by Mithra).

The Magi's appearance was not coincidental; it was an anticipation of their longstanding tradition of following "the shining star" on Dec 21, expecting the birth of their next Saoshyant (Messiah). They presented three highly symbolic gifts from their Persian heritage: gold, frankincense, and myrrh. Gold symbolized **Zar**athustra (as "Zar" means gold in Persian), while frankincense had religious significance in Zoroastrian ceremonies since ancient times. Myrrh, used for body preservation, was offered to anoint and bless Yeshua for his mission. Even today, frankincense and myrrh continue to be offered at Zoroastrian fire altars.

It is important to note that certain verses in The Gathas, Zarathustra's sacred hymns about the coming of the Saoshyants/Messiah, were written over 2000 years before Yeshua's (Jesus') birth. To gain a deeper understanding of the Magi's role in Yeshua's life and ministry, we should explore the concept of the Messiah in both Judaism and Zoroastrianism. Comparing their differences and expectations regarding the Messiah could provide insights into why Yeshua's birth and mission were embraced by the Magi but met with rejection by his Jewish contemporaries.

Perhaps the story of the Magi (Zoroastrian priests) in the Gospel is symbolic—a parable. Maybe Matthew wanted to highlight that "a prophet is not welcomed in his own hometown." The Persians might have recognized and celebrated the birth of a savior (Saoshyant) as predicted by their prophet Zarathustra, showing more acceptance and acknowledgment than Christ's own people.

While Romans followed Paganism and Mithraism, both Jews and Persians held Messianic beliefs during Yeshua's time, anticipating their respective Messiahs. However, the concept of the Messiah differed significantly between Persian Zoroastrians and Jews at that time.

CHAPTER 2

Influence of Zoroastrianism on Judaism

King Cyrus: Jewish messiah

This is what the LORD says to Cyrus, his appointed king: "I hold your right hand and will help you defeat nations and take away other kings' power. I will open doors for you so city gates will not stop you. I will go before you and make the mountains flat.

Isaiah 45:1-4

Zoroastrianism was a prominent religion in the Persian empire from the 6th century BCE to the 7th century CE. Many scholars believe that Zoroastrian concepts and beliefs influenced Judaism from its early stages and later impacted Christianity, Islam, Bahai, and even certain aspects of northern Buddhism and Gnostic faiths. Key concepts like heaven, hell, the immortality of the soul, the Last Judgment, rewards and punishments in the afterlife, redemption, the idea of a Saoshyant (Messiah), the existence of an evil spirit (Ahriman), Paradise, and the presence of angels and demons can trace their origins back to the teachings of Zarathustra.

> *The idea of a single god was not the only essentially Zoroastrian tenet that found its way into other major faiths, most notably the 'big three': Judaism, Christianity, and Islam. The concepts of Heaven and Hell, Judgment Day and the final revelation of the world, and angels and demons all originated in the teachings of Zarathustra, as well as the later canon of Zoroastrian literature they inspired. Even the idea of Satan is a fundamentally Zoroastrian one; in fact, the entire faith of Zoroastrianism is predicated on the struggle between God and the forces of goodness and light (represented by the Holy Spirit, Spenta Manyu) and Ahriman, who presides over the forces of darkness and evil. While man has to choose to which side he belongs, the religion teaches that ultimately, God will prevail, and even those condemned to hellfire will enjoy the blessings of Paradise (an Old Persian word).*[23]

The Jewish people resided in Jerusalem under the Kingdom of Judah for a significant period before the city fell. In 586 BCE, the Babylonian Empire besieged Jerusalem after years of conflict. The city was conquered, leading to the destruction of houses, the burning of the sacred temple, and the deportation of many prominent Jewish citizens and artisans to Babylon. Judah then became a Babylonian province, marking the start of the Jewish exile from their homeland. *And he burnt the house of the LORD,*

---

[23] *Bekhrad, Joobin. "The Obscure Religion that Shaped the West." BBC Culture, April 6, 2017.*
https://www.bbc.com/culture/article/20170406-this-obscure-religion-shaped-the-west

and the king's house; and all the houses of Jerusalem, and every great man's house, burnt with fire.[24]

The Jewish exile in Babylon persisted for many years until the Persians, heavily influenced by Zoroastrianism, conquered Babylon in 539 BCE under the leadership of King Cyrus. This event fulfilled the prophecy of Isaiah regarding the liberation of the Jews from captivity. King Cyrus was hailed as the Jewish messiah, or the anointed one.

The period of Persian influence on Judaism, spanning almost two centuries, was a crucial historical phase that left a lasting impact on the Old Testament and Jewish culture. The rule of King Cyrus and his successors differed significantly from that of previous captors like the Assyrians, Babylonians, and Egyptians.

Then they (Persians) gave money to the masons and carpenters, and gave food and drink and olive oil to the people of Sidon and Tyre, so that they would bring cedar logs by sea from Lebanon to Joppa, as authorized by Cyrus king of Persia."[25]

Unlike other conquerors who kept their captives far from their homelands and enslaved them, the Persians took a different approach with the Jews. They facilitated their return to their homeland, supported them in rebuilding their Temple using funds from the Persian treasury, and assisted in collecting their sacred scriptures from various locations across the Persian Empire. This contrasted sharply with the actions of

---

[24] *2 King 25:9-10. KJV*

[25] *Ezra 3:7. NIV*

the Babylonians, who had previously destroyed much of the Jewish heritage.

> *2 This is what Cyrus, king of Persia, says:*
>
> *"The Lord, the God of heaven, has given me all the kingdoms of the earth and he has appointed me to build a temple for him at Jerusalem in Judah. 3 Any of his people among you may go up to Jerusalem in Judah and build the temple of the Lord, the God of Israel, the God who is in Jerusalem, and may their God be with them. 4 And in any locality where survivors may now be living, the people are to provide them with silver and gold, with goods and livestock, and with freewill offerings for the temple of God in Jerusalem."*[26]

Zoroastrianism was rooted in the principle of tolerance towards other religions and spiritual beliefs. Zarathustra advocated that no one should be coerced or forced into converting to Zoroastrianism; rather, faith should be chosen freely, consciously, and willingly. The liberation of the Jews from the Babylon captivity by Persians brought a major shift in the Jewish faith.

All religions build on earlier traditions, and Judaism is no different. It incorporates ideas from ancient Iran, such as angels, demons, light and darkness, God, and an Adversary. These influences are evident in Jewish writings about the End of Time and a final Judgment by God, reflecting Zoroastrian beliefs.

Cyrus' decree allowed the Jews to return to their homeland, build their Temple, and return the article taken by Babaylon to the sacred Temple.

---

[26] *Ezra 1:2-3. NIV*

> 13 However, in the first year of Cyrus king of Babylon, King Cyrus issued a decree to rebuild this house of God. 14 He even removed from the temple of Babylon the gold and silver articles of the house of God, which Nebuchadnezzar had taken from the temple in Jerusalem and brought to the temple in Babylon. Then King Cyrus gave them to a man named Sheshbazzar, whom he had appointed governor, 15 and he told him, 'Take these articles and go and deposit them in the temple in Jerusalem. And rebuild the house of God on its site.'[27]

King Cyrus was not the sole supporter of the Jews; some of his successors from the Achaemenid dynasty also provided support and protection to the Jewish community. The initial return of the Jews started during the reign of Darius I, while the second return from exile to Jerusalem took place under the rule of Artaxerxes I, who governed Babylon from 465 to 424 B.C.

> 14 So the elders of the Jews continued to build and prosper under the preaching of Haggai the prophet and Zechariah, a descendant of Iddo. They finished building the temple according to the command of the God of Israel and the decrees of Cyrus, Darius and Artaxerxes, kings of Persia.[28]

Despite the opportunity to return, not all Jews were eager to go back to Jerusalem. After living in exile for around sixty years, many Jews had settled and integrated into Babylonian society, becoming accustomed to their new environment. Some chose to stay in Babylon, where they thrived in various fields, such as business and politics, under the Persian Empire. In fact, a few

---

[27] Ezra 5:13-15. NIV

[28] Ezra 6:14. NIV

prominent Jews even attained positions of importance within the Persian court.

The story of Esther illustrates the life of a young Jewish woman living in the Persian Kingdom during the 4th century B.C. She was named Hadassah and was chosen by King Xerxes I to become Queen of Persia, receiving the name Esther from the king. Esther originates from an old Persian girl's name, "stāra," which means "star." Esther's influence on the king was so profound that she courageously risked her life to protect her people, the Jews, from persecution orchestrated by the Persian Prime Minister, Haman.

10 King Xerxes imposed tribute throughout the empire, to its distant shores. 2 And all his acts of power and might, together with a full account of the greatness of Mordecai, whom the king had promoted, are not written in the book of the annals of the kings of Media and Persia? 3 Mordecai the Jew was second in rank to King Xerxes, preeminent among the Jews, and held in high esteem by his many fellow Jews, because he worked for the good of his people and spoke up for the welfare of all the Jews.[29]

After the Jews were liberated and returned to their homeland in post-exilic Judaism, those who had been living among Persians experienced significant cultural exchange. This interaction led to changes in the Jewish religion, prompting a substantial revision after the exile ended. A new ideology about God emerged from Zoroastrianism, influencing Judaism. This period also saw the emergence of distinct groups within Judaism, such

---

[29] Esther 10. NIV

as the Sadducees and Pharisees, who held differing beliefs and interpretations of religious practices.

Savior or Messiah

The idea of a savior or Messiah emerging to free humanity from evil greatly impacted Judaism, thanks to Zoroastrian influence. In Jewish belief, the Messiah, or anointed one, is someone chosen by God to rescue and liberate the Jewish people, even if they are not Jewish, akin to King Cyrus. This Persian influence on Judaism becomes evident in the Book of Second Isaiah, written during and after the Exile, which prophesied the coming of a Jewish Messiah resembling King Cyrus. For centuries, the concept of the Messiah, known as Saoshyant in Zoroastrianism, had already existed in Zarathustra's holy book, The Gathas, describing Saoshyant as a benefactor for all of humanity.

Messiah in Judaism

> *This is what the Lord says to his anointed,*
> *to Cyrus, whose right hand I take hold of*
> *to subdue nations before him*
> *and to strip kings of their armor,*
> *to open doors before him*
> *so that gates will not be shut:*
> *I will go before you*
> *and will level the mountains[a];*
> *I will break down gates of bronze*
> *and cut through bars of iron.*
> *I will give you hidden treasures,*
> *riches stored in secret places,*

THE MESSIAH: SAOSHYANT

*so that you may know that I am the Lord,
the God of Israel, who summons you by name.*[30]

In the Jewish tradition, God promised the coming of the Messiah for the people of Israel. According to professor Mary Boyce "The Verses of IInd Isaiah are remarkable in that in them alone, out of all the Old Testament, the term 'Messiah' in the sense of an anointed deliverer of the Jewish nation is used of foreigner, a non-Jew (Cyrus)."[31] The term "Messiah" or "Anointed One" is mentioned throughout the Old Testament, with early indications in Genesis (3:15) and multiple references in Psalms and Isaiah. In older Jewish scriptures, the Messiah was often referred to as any king of the Jews who was considered an "Anointed One." These "Anointed Ones," like King David, were believed to possess "God-given power." The Messiah was also expected to be a physical descendant of the Davidic line, specifically through King David[32] and King Solomon.

At the time of Yeshua (Jesus), the land of the Jews was under Roman rule. Many Jews were expecting a messiah to come and fight for them against the Romans, similar to how King Cyrus liberated them from Babylon. Alternatively, they were waiting for a prophet like Moses to free them from oppression, as Moses had freed them from slavery in Egypt.

The idea of the Messiah in the first century was quite different from what Yeshua (Jesus) was preaching. Many Jews expected a Messiah who would liberate Israel from Roman oppressors and lead them to freedom, not a simple rabbi and carpenter

---

[30] *Isaiah, 45:1-3*

[31] Boyce, Mary. *A History of Zoroastrianism, Volume II.* Brill, 1982., p. 44.

[32] *Jeremiah 23:5, Isaiah 11:1-4*

from Galilee. Yeshua seemed too loving and peaceful, lacking the qualities of a military commander. Additionally, he continuously challenged the Pharisees and their corruption, which did not align with the Jews' expectations for their Messiah. Consequently, his people did not welcome his mission and challenges.

Messiah in Zoroastrianism

> *When will Mazda's bright dawn of victory embrace the world? When will the radiance of the sun shine upon all the lands? When will the Saoshyants (Saviors) become numerous, spreading the faith through their deeds and actions? Now a Saoshyant stands to teach the people, and I, Zarathustra, follow you, O Ahura.*[33]

The Gathas, the sacred hymns of Zarathustra, speak of a future Savior sent by Ahura Mazda (The Supreme Being) called Saoshyant. This term means "the one who brings benefit" to humankind and is prophesied to lead righteousness over wickedness. During the Parthian period, the Magi were anticipating the arrival of their Saoshyant and were watching the skies as astrologers for a sign of his appearance, symbolized by a shining star (Zarathustra – the shining, bright star). At the time of Yeshua, Persians were not waiting for a savior to rescue them from captivity, as they had already established a vast empire under the Zoroastrian religion. Instead, they were expecting a Saoshyant to be born to guide them and bring the message of Ahura Mazda to humanity.

In contrast to the Judaic idea of the Messiah, Zarathustra's concept of the Saoshyant was not focused on saving any

---

[33] The Gathas, 46-3

particular nation or ethnic group. Instead, the mission of the Saoshyant was to guide all of humanity toward a happier and more joyful life on Earth. The Saoshyant would come to complete Zarathustra's mission and make the Earth like Heaven. The verses from Zarathustra in the Gathas, regarding the coming of the Messiah, were written at least 2,000 years before Yeshua's birth.

According to Zarathustra in the Gathas:

Those who oppose idol worshipers and their followers, as well as those who remember the name of the Lord with goodness and honor the wise Saoshyants and helpers of the true religion, Mazda Ahura will treat them with sincere friendship, brotherhood, and compassionate fatherhood. Their path is completely separate from those who belittle the unity of Mazda Ahura and remember Him with ugliness.[34]

Indeed, the Soshyants and the saviors of the world will be those who, by following good thoughts, fulfill their duty.[35]

O Mazda, show me the true path of good thoughts. Also, inform Soshyant (the savior) of the reward for his work.[36]

With the guidance of *Soashyants* (guides, saviors), humanity will make the Earth like a paradise again. Humanity will regain "the golden age" of the original creation of peace and prosperity on Earth. Zarathustra was a *Soashyant*,[37] a savior of humanity to guide us toward healthier and more conscious

---

[34] Yasna 45-11

[35] Yasna 48-12

[36] Yasna 48-9

[37] Yasna 50.11, Yasna 29.6-11

life on Earth. He hoped that this restoration would occur by the end of his life.[38] However, he also pointed out that other *Soashyants* and saviors would come after him to complete his mission and teachings on Earth.

Frashokereti - A final restoration of the universe to its origin of Paradise (perfection)

Some saviors (Soashyants) will come to guide humanity towards peace and perfection again.

---

[38] Yasna 48.2, Yasna 34.15, Yasna 46.19

CHAPTER 3

Esoteric vs. Exoteric knowledge

Zarathustra's mission was not to establish another religion but to promote a new concept of God and spirituality different from what existed in his time. He opposed enslaving human souls to dogmatic beliefs or robotic worship. Instead, he aimed to break the chains of ignorance and deception that entangled humanity in unconsciousness. His teachings were not about creating a belief system to follow blindly; rather, they encouraged people to actively grow their consciousness towards Divine Consciousness.

After the death of Zarathustra, his ideas continued along two main paths: Zoroastrian religion and Zoroastrian mysticism, also known as Mazdaism. These two main paths gradually evolved in later times and had extensive influences on human thought and philosophy.

1. Zoroastrian Religion (**Zoroastrianism**): This path continued Zarathustra's religious teachings, maintaining adherence to the principles and religious rituals of Zoroastrianism. This included beliefs in the one God (Ahura Mazda), the concept of the dualistic struggle between good and evil (Ahura Mazda and Angra Mainyu), ethics, and making the best choices to achieve happiness and worldly and otherworldly salvation, as well as

the Gregorian calendar, celebrations, and religious ceremonies related to Zoroastrian rituals.

2. Zarathustra's Mysticism or Mazdaism (**Mazda-Yasna**): The principles of Zarathustra's mysticism continued as one of the paths of thought and philosophy after Zarathustra's death. These principles were profoundly influenced not only by Greek philosophers like Pythagoras, Aristotle, and Plato but also by Jewish mysticism (Kabbalah), a part of Buddhist mysticism, and Islamic mysticism (Sufism) such as Suhrawardi. The term "philosophy" is derived from the meaning "love of wisdom" from "Mazda Yasna."

This term dates back to ancient Greece, and the term "philosopher" refers to individuals who seek knowledge, truth, and wisdom. The term "Mazdaism," derived from Zarathustra's language, means "followers of wisdom" or "lovers of wisdom." It refers more to individuals who seek truths, deeper understandings of realities, and intellectual and spiritual development. In general, the terms "philosophy" and "Mazdaism" signify the search for truth and wisdom. In the context of Zarathustra's mysticism, known as Mazda Yasna, emphasis has been placed on principles that focus on inner work and human self-actualization. The intention of this book, as mentioned earlier, is to explore the esoteric teachings of Zarathustra based on Mazdaism (Mazda-Yasna) rather than the Zoroastrian religion.

Being is our true nature, and to achieve this transformation, just existing and being content with who we are is not enough to bring this inner alchemy. The teachings of Mazdaism focus on inner work and are passed down through oral tradition. This wisdom has been shared orally over centuries since

Zarathustra's time. The Magi, who were close to Zarathustra, learned directly from him and shared his wisdom to others for centuries.

Esoteric knowledge is centered around spiritual or philosophical truths that have a hidden meaning than the outer. The teaching is often taught through symbols, stories, metaphor and allegory to deliver deeper meanings that are not obvious in the surface-level understanding. The stories have layers of meanings beyond their literal interpretation.

> *Jesus used stories to tell all these things to the people. He always used stories to teach them. This was to make clear the full meaning of what the prophet said: "I will speak using stories; I will tell things that have been secrets since the world was made.*[39]

Esoteric teachings are intended for a select few who have been initiated, trained, or possess a deep understanding of the subject. For instance, Yeshua had his twelve apostles to whom he explained the inner meanings of his parables, while most people only grasped the literal interpretations of his wisdom. When morning came, he called his disciples to him and chose twelve of them, whom he also designated apostles.[9] After giving his sermons to the public, Yeshua often gathered his disciples to teach them the deeper, esoteric meanings of his wisdom.

> *Then he left the crowd and went into the house. His disciples came to him and said, "Explain to us the parable of the weeds in the field.*[40]

---

[39] Matthew 13 ERV

[40] Matthew 13:36 NIV

Similarly, Zarathustra had seven Magi in his inner circle to whom he taught the deeper meaning of his teachings. This esoteric knowledge provides a more profound and hidden aspect of spirituality that is not easily accessible to the general public. The path of Mazdaism focuses the inner teachings and esoteric wisdom of Zarathustra, which have been passed down orally through centuries by the Magi.

Exoteric knowledge is available to everyone, regardless of their background or experience. It includes basic teachings that believers can follow without special initiation. This type of knowledge provides a simple understanding and the literal meanings of the subject, helping followers practice their faith externally. It offers a common framework and principles to guide people toward righteousness and virtuous living, aiming to reach a wide audience with straightforward teachings and rituals.

Mazdaism (Mazda-Yasna): Mazda means wisdom, and Mazdaism refers to following wisdom and consciousness. It is not a religion but a path focused on evolving and maturing as a human being. Mazdaism rejects herd mentality and emphasizes individual wisdom and awareness. It does not involve dull rituals or superstitious ideas but promotes growth and wisdom. The path of Mazda aims to increase one's awareness over time to live more wisely. It is a journey of liberation and making conscious choices to create possibilities and fulfill our higher potential as human beings.

According to Zarathustra, all humans are created "Good" out of love and wisdom. Therefore, one must first find wisdom and goodness within themselves and continuously cultivate these qualities throughout life. Zarathustra consistently challenged superstition, corruption, and deception from spiritual and political leaders. In his book, the Gathas, there are no irrational, pessimistic, dogmatic, or superstitious statements. He urged people to listen to him consciously and not follow his words blindly out of obligation or pressure. He believed in the freedom to choose one's path wisely. His teachings focus on esoteric knowledge and the inner transformation from a lower to a higher self and consciousness.

Zarathustra's moral values are based on one's level of consciousness (Mazda) and conscience (Daena). His morality is rooted in "pure consciousness." He encourages people to act out of awareness rather than blind obedience. In his terms, good means thoughts, words, and actions that arise from awareness, while bad (evil) means those that arise from ignorance and unconsciousness. Zarathustra transcends concepts of purity and impurity, right and wrong. Mazda and wisdom go beyond these dualities. Virtue that comes from ignorance is merely hypocrisy because it does not arise from one's inner light.

Both Zarathustra and Yeshua (Jesus) continuously targeted the hypocrisy of the religious leaders of their times. Both were ultimately killed by these hypocritical, virtuous priests. According to Zarathustra, virtue should be based on one's intelligence, logic, and wisdom. A key element of Zarathustra's vision is free will, emphasizing the moral responsibility of the individual. Every decision people make is an opportunity to serve either "Good" (Mazda, light, and consciousness) or "Bad" (Ahriman, darkness, and unconsciousness).

Zarathustra stresses that as humans, we have the freedom to choose between living consciously or unconsciously. This choice allows us to understand the difference between wisdom

(Mazda) and ignorance (Ahriman). Each decision we make contributes to one of these two sides. Consciousness is our ability to discern between "good" and "bad," setting us apart from animals with limited moral sense or free will. Our freedom of choice empowers us to align with our conscious side or with ignorance. In Zarathustra's perspective, religion (Deen, Daena) represents our inner conscience.

Both Yeshua (Jesus) and Zarathustra emphasized that all "sins" originate from ignorance. They viewed the Divine as the Ultimate Consciousness, while Ahriman (Satan) represented a state of ignorance. Yeshua's famous words, *Father, forgive them, for they do not know what they are doing,*[41] illustrate his compassion and understanding toward people acting out of ignorance. Despite facing insults and harm, Yeshua chose forgiveness because he recognized the root cause behind their actions. His pure heart and deep wisdom led him to show mercy even in the face of adversity, such as during his crucifixion.

Zarathustra and Yeshua both taught us to think carefully before acting, choosing goodness over badness and guarding our minds from negativity. Zarathustra stresses that Mazda granted us consciousness to discern between good and bad, right and wrong. Humans aren't meant to be mechanical; we're here to learn and consciously decide our thoughts, words, and actions. Likewise, Yeshua teaches us to be conscious and awake in guarding our minds against negative thoughts, likening them to weeds that can spread and affect our inner selves, which should be nurtured with positive thoughts and intentions.

---

[41] Luke 23:34

THE MESSIAH: SAOSHYANT

Jesus told them another parable: "The kingdom of heaven is like a man who sowed good seed in his field. 25 But while everyone was sleeping, his enemy came and sowed weeds among the wheat, and went away. 26 When the wheat sprouted and formed heads, then the weeds also appeared.[42]

Zarathustra and enlightened teachers wake us from ignorance and guide us to divine awareness. They help us see, hear, and understand deeper truths. Just like Yeshua metaphorically brings the dead to life, they awaken us to a new level of living through awareness. They came to heal our inner sight and hearing, not just to listen superficially, but to comprehend deeply. *So that, they may be ever seeing but never perceiving, and ever hearing but never understanding; otherwise they might turn and be forgiven!*[43]

Zarathustra didn't look at Ahura Mazda in the sky or heaven. He was like a deep-sea diver, seeking the pearl within the depths of his consciousness. He delved so profoundly inward to discover his true essence. And in that depth, he found no one but God, realizing that his true self was nothing but Ahura Mazda.

O Mazda, when I saw You in my mind, I realized that You are the wisdom of the entire world.[44]

Since I have seen Ahura Mazda with my inner eyes.[45]

---

[42] Matthew 13:24-26, NIV

[43] Mark 4:12, NIV

[44] Yasna 31-8

[45] Yasna 45-8

Zarathustra didn't rely on belief or faith to know God; he explored the divine within himself. He urges others to delve into their own depths to discover the Divine (Ahura Mazda) within their vast consciousness. His knowledge of God stemmed not from external observation but from inner perception within the depths of his consciousness. Similarly, Yeshua says:

> *For indeed, the kingdom of God is within you.*[46]

As time passes, we come to understand that mere survival and material accumulation are insufficient. An existential yearning and desire develop within us, indicating a deeper purpose on Earth beyond mere existence, accumulation, and self-preservation. Each individual carries an inherent void that cannot be filled by material possessions or technological progress. This void is unique to humans and sets us apart from other beings in the universe. Our existence is not limited to basic survival; we have a profound purpose to fulfill ourselves holistically, both outwardly and inwardly. As Zarathustra states in the Gathas,

> *Oh, Ahura Mazda, I turn to you with good thoughts. In the light of truth, grant me blessings in both the material and spiritual worlds, leading people to happiness.*[47]

Similarly, Yeshua preached the same message:

> *Jesus answered, "It is written: 'Man shall not live on bread alone, but on every word that comes from the mouth of God.'"*[48]

---

[46] Luke 17:21 NKJV

[47] Yasna 28-2

[48] Matthew 4:4. NIV

What good will it be for someone to gain the whole world, yet forfeit their soul? Or what can anyone give in exchange for their soul?[49]

Being "born again" refers to an awakening where individuals rediscover their true essence beyond their personalities. This process involves becoming aware of one's authentic self, often referred to as the faravashi or Essence, and striving to develop it towards a divine state. It signifies a shift in life's focus from the horizontal (linear, physical existence marked by birth, death, and time-based past, present, future) to the vertical (eternity, spiritual, and divine realms). This awakening, also known as Self-Remembering, marks a profound shift in consciousness.

Jesus replied, "Very truly I tell you, no one can see the kingdom of God unless they are born again.[50]

At a certain stage in life, the linear growth and identification with our personality may cease to provide fulfillment. This is when we turn inward to rediscover the essence we left behind, often around the age of four, and begin to nurture and grow that essence. It's important to note that our essence, also known as faravashi, initially exists as a seed. We have the potential to cultivate this essence deeper within ourselves and strive towards transforming from ignorance to higher wisdom and consciousness. Similar to Zarathustra, Yeshua also urged people to return to the seed of their essence as a pathway towards reaching the Kingdom of heaven.

---

[49] Matthew 16:26, NIV

[50] John 3:3. NIV

And he said: "Truly I tell you, unless you change and become like little children, you will never enter the kingdom of heaven."[51]

We are not just here to have a selfish life. Rather, we are also here to help other human beings in their inner and outer growth in life. *"Happiness belongs to those who make others happy."*[52] This Zarathustra's statement is also parallel with Yeshua's teaching: *"Love your neighbor as yourself."*[53]

We need the teaching and guidance of enlightened masters like Buddha, Zarathustra, or Yeshua to help us attain higher wisdom and consciousness. Zarathustra, with his mission from Mazda, sought to guide humanity toward wisdom.[54] And those who follow his teachings will be guided by the Good Mind, which leads them to good deeds.[55]

Yeshua taught similarly as well: *"When Jesus spoke again to the people, he said, "I am the light of the world. Whoever follows me will never walk in darkness, but will have the light of life."*[56]

The mind often becomes an obstacle when it prevents us from seeing things through the eyes of consciousness. It acts like a dark cloud covering the light of consciousness. Unless we examine the nature of our minds and dissolve these barriers, we cannot go deeper within or see the truth as it is. Hopefully, there comes a point in our lives when we start questioning what

---

[51] Matthew 18:3. NIV

[52] Yasna 43-1

[53] Matthew 22:39

[54] Yasna 29-8

[55] Yasna 45-5

[56] John 8:12, NIV

THE MESSIAH: SAOSHYANT

our environment has instilled in us. In Zen, this is referred to as finding our original face.

There comes a point in our lives when we no longer accept things blindly or believe based on ignorance, fears, or rewards. We start to examine everything we know with pure consciousness and wisdom. This means becoming like a child again, looking at everything with curiosity and wonder. At this point, we need to destroy the temple of our mind and rebuild it, as we can't build on top of a corrupted foundation. We must let go of everything we know and rebuild from scratch, like resetting a phone to its factory settings.

The purpose of human creation is not suffering; we are here to live joyful and happy lives on Earth. Zarathustra taught that we are not meant to endure suffering on Earth and then enjoy life in Heaven after death. Instead, we are born to make Earth like Heaven while we are alive. This is why gardening was important in most ancient Zoroastrian homes, serving as a reminder and symbol of Heaven on Earth for his followers.

The mission of the future Saoshyant (Savior) in Zarathustra's view was not to save any particular nation or ethnic group. Instead, the purpose of the Saoshyant was to guide humanity toward a happier and joyful life free from corruption and deception. The Saoshyant would come to complete Zarathustra's mission to make Earth like Heaven.

Similar to Zarathustra's life, Yeshua's ministry focused on challenging the corruption and deceptions around him.

Then Jesus said to the crowds and to his disciples: 2"The teachers of the law and the Pharisees sit in Moses' seat. 3 So you must be careful to do everything they tell you. But do not do what they do, for they do not practice what they preach."[57]

He consistently challenged people, including the Pharisees, urging them to follow their path consciously rather than blindly. He faced criticism for activities such as eating, working, and healing on the Sabbath. *Then he said to them, 'The Sabbath was made for man, not man for the Sabbath. So the son of Man is Lord even of the Sabbath.'*[58] Yeshua, similar to Zarathustra's approach to life, lived with a spirit of feasting and celebration. His joyful attitude toward life often drew criticism from others. *They said to him, "John's disciples often fast and pray, and so do the disciples of the Pharisees, but yours go on eating and drinking."*[59]

Yeshua, like Zarathustra, emphasized principles of "Good Thoughts, Good Words, and Good Deeds." When questioned about his moral stance on eating during the Sabbath, he often challenged the Pharisees' rigid interpretations. *What goes into someone's mouth does not defile them, but what comes out of their mouth, that is what defiles them.*[60] Yeshua taught his disciples about a loving and forgiving God. One of his central teachings was that *Whoever does not love does not know God, because God is love.*[61]

---

[57] Matthew 23:1-3

[58] Mark 2:2t-28

[59] Luke 5:33

[60] Matthew 15:11

[61] John 4:8

Throughout his life and ministry, Yeshua consistently emphasized the attributes of a loving and forgiving God. He taught his followers through parables, direct teachings, and his own actions that God's love and forgiveness are central to spiritual life and relationships. Yeshua's life itself was a powerful example of the compassion, mercy, and forgiveness that he preached, demonstrating these qualities in his interactions with people from all walks of life. His teachings and actions continue to inspire and guide people seeking spiritual truth and understanding today.

CONCLUSION

Zarathustra's wisdom has indeed had a profound and lasting impact across different cultures and belief systems throughout history. His teachings on truth, righteousness, and the pursuit of wisdom have resonated with various civilizations, influencing not only religious thought but also ethical and philosophical perspectives.

Today, as we navigate through complex global challenges and societal changes, the principles of Mazdaism—focused on truth, conscious choice, and the pursuit of goodness—remain relevant. By embracing these teachings in our daily lives, we can contribute to creating a more enlightened and compassionate world. Just as Zarathustra illuminated his era, we too can strive to bring clarity and integrity into our present-day interactions and decisions, thereby fostering harmony and understanding in our communities and beyond.

The Magi morality centers on principles of goodness and personal choice. Zarathustra did not advocate for people to abandon their existing religions, cultures, or traditions. Instead, he envisioned unification through wisdom and goodness. Zarathustra taught the harmonization of life guided by the principles of "Good Thoughts, Good Words, and Good Deeds," encouraging individuals to pursue ethical conduct and spiritual growth irrespective of their diverse cultural backgrounds.

Zarathustra's verses in the Gathas reflect his inner dialogue, a conversation within his own conscious mind. Mythological interpretations have portrayed these dialogues and questions as interactions with an external entity named Ahura Mazda. However, Zarathustra viewed Mazda not as an external being, but as a mental construct symbolizing profound human wisdom.

Throughout history, humanity has often lived like a herd, following traditions, rules, and principles unconsciously. However, there have always been individuals who challenged this norm and awakened humanity to higher purposes. Their lives were guided not by external forces but by their own intelligence and individuality. These individuals did not seek to revolutionize society, but rather risked everything to attain ultimate freedom from our bondages and conditionings.

In consumerist societies, there's often a greater emphasis on pursuing happiness rather than finding meaning in life. Happiness is often linked to personal comfort and feeling good. However, when happiness lacks a foundation in higher values and meaning, it can lead to a shallow, self-centered existence. Pursuing happiness without deeper meaning can make one selfish, focused only on fulfilling personal needs and desires.

In the midst of today's chaotic world, what we truly need isn't more division, hatred, or greed. Humanity craves unity and wisdom. We must seek universal principles and values that can unite us and guide us towards becoming loving, conscious beings. It's crucial to show compassion towards our planet and all its living creatures. We find ourselves still imprisoned by ignorance, vanity, deception, and greed. To break free, we must support each other, devise a map and plan, and have leadership to guide us toward liberation. We can also draw upon the wisdom of enlightened masters who have already escaped this unconscious prison.

Many saviors like Zarathustra, Buddha, and Yeshua sought to free humanity from ignorance. Yeshua's teachings in the Gospels resonate deeply with Zarathustra's wisdom in the Gathas. Yeshua's teachings resonated with Zarathustra's view of a Loving, Good, and Wise Lord. He aimed to bring "Good News" centered on goodness: Good Thoughts, Good Words, Good Deeds.

Both Zarathustra and Yeshua employed metaphorical teachings to convey deeper spiritual truths. Yeshua's parable of transforming water into wine in the Gospel of John[32] illustrates this beautifully, symbolizing the inner transformation from a basic state to a higher spiritual state. Similarly, in Persian Sufism, wine often symbolizes divine wisdom, with the act of drinking it metaphorically representing spiritual intoxication and enlightenment. Persian mystics like Hafiz often used such metaphors, likening esoteric knowledge to the experience of a tavern where spiritual seekers imbibe divine truths.

> *Whoever had found his way to the tavern's block*
> *Would have to be insane if on another door knock*
> *Fate never crowned any with drunkenness, except*
> *The one who considered this the highest luck.*
> *Whoever finds his way into the tavern*
> *From the bounty of the wine, temple's secrets unlock.*
> *He who read the secrets of this wine,*
> *Found the secrets in the dust upon which we walk.*[62]

---

[62] *Hafiz*, Ghazal 47

The parable of turning water into wine signifies a profound transformation from the ordinary truth to a higher Truth beyond what is initially perceived. It represents the journey towards understanding "the truth of Truth," where one transcends from a basic state (water) to a spiritually elevated state (wine). This transformation mirrors the caterpillar's metamorphosis into a butterfly, symbolizing a complete change in form and essence, reflecting inner growth and spiritual evolution.

Yeshua's teachings were about focusing on spiritual growth and inner transformation rather than worldly achievements or material concerns. The idea of the Kingdom of Heaven, as he taught it, emphasized an inner state of being rather than external material success or achievements. This spiritual dimension encouraged people to seek a deeper connection with their higher selves and Higher Being. *The kingdom of God is in the midst of you.*[63]

Yeshua, like Zarathustra and many other spiritual teachers, spoke metaphorically about the transformation of the self from a lower state to a higher, more spiritually evolved state—similar to the alchemical process of turning base metals into gold. The Kingdom of Heaven, in this context, represents not just a place but a state of being that one achieves through inner evolution and transformation towards a higher spiritual consciousness.

Just as an apple seed has the potential to grow into an apple tree and a house requires construction to become a home, Yeshua and Zarathustra both used metaphors to illustrate the process of inner transformation. Yeshua's reference to destroying and rebuilding the temple can be understood as a metaphor

---

[63] Luke 17:21

for shedding old, limiting beliefs and behaviors to cultivate a new, spiritually enlightened self. Similarly, Zarathustra's idea of creating a "new character" emphasizes the continuous process of self-development and evolution towards wisdom, consciousness, and goodness. This journey involves taking responsibility for our own growth and transformation, much like being both the land and the builder of our own spiritual house.

When Yeshua spoke of being "poor in spirit," he wasn't advocating literal poverty or deprivation but rather a state of humility, detachment from ego, and a focus on inner spiritual wealth. This contrasts with being "rich in personality," where one identifies strongly with external traits and material possessions, potentially obstructing deeper spiritual growth. The Kingdom of Heaven, in this context, is accessible to those who cultivate inner wisdom and spiritual awareness, transcending the limitations of mere material or superficial identities.

In Eastern spirituality, wise individuals are often referred to as "mad-men," "drunkards," or "beggars" because they symbolically embody humility and a profound desire for wisdom. This portrayal emphasizes their recognition of spiritual poverty compared to the vastness of Wisdom (often symbolized as a King, such as Mazda in Persian literature). When Yeshua says "Blessed are the poor," he speaks to those who acknowledge their spiritual poverty and actively seek inner wisdom. This understanding highlights that esoteric teachings often contain both literal and deeper psychological or spiritual meanings, inviting seekers to explore profound truths about existence and the path to spiritual fulfillment.

In spiritual terms, a "rich person" in spirit can be seen as someone who is spiritually ignorant or unaware. Such individuals may be overly absorbed in their own ego, consumed by the various voices and concerns of their personality. This preoccupation with self-centered thoughts, judgments, complaints, and self-importance can create a barrier that prevents them from being open to receiving wisdom or higher truths. In this state, they may metaphorically be described as blind to deeper insights and deaf to spiritual guidance, as they focus solely on their inner chatter and desires. Thus, being "rich in spirit" in this context signifies a lack of spiritual receptivity and a dominance of ego-driven perceptions and behaviors.

The Pharisees

Every person always has two sides: the inner and the outer. The inner part is our emotion, thoughts, and consciousness. No one knows exactly what you think or feel except you. You cannot measure your inner world by its weight, smell, touch, visual, or test. In therapy, dreams are important because they show our deeper feelings and thoughts symbolically.

Spiritual rebirth, like Yeshua talked about, means waking up to a deeper understanding of ourselves beyond just everyday life. It's like realizing our true essence, like finding the "Master of the house" inside us, even when life's distractions try to pull us away. This journey is about discovering our inner world and growing in spiritual awareness, going beyond what we can measure or see on the surface.

The outer part of ourselves is what others see—our physical appearance, financial situation, possessions like cars or homes, our clothing, and even our professions. These external aspects often shape initial impressions and judgments about us. When Yeshua advises "Judge not," he urges us not to assess others solely based on these external factors or our own internal biases and preconceptions. Instead, he encourages seeing beyond appearances to understand the person within. This concept aligns with the practice of empathy in therapy and compassion in spirituality—both emphasize connecting with others on a deeper, more meaningful level, beyond superficial judgments or outward appearances.

Once, there was a mystic who returned to a village after many months of meditation in the mountains. He appeared disheveled, wearing dirty clothes and looking poor. The villagers did not recognize him and treated him like a beggar, feeding him reluctantly and keeping their distance.

A year later, the mystic returned to the same village, but this time he was well-groomed and presented himself neatly. Immediately, the villagers welcomed him warmly, prepared a feast in his honour, and eagerly served him gourmet food.

During the feast, the mystic surprised everyone by removing his coat, shirt, and hat and feeding gourmet food to his clothes. Puzzled, someone asked him, "Why are you feeding your clothes and disrespecting our food?"

The mystic calmly replied, "A year ago, when I came here looking poor, no one fed or sheltered me because I did not appear as you expected. Now, you are feeding me not for who I am, but for how I appear. I am the same person as before, unchanged inside. So, I thank my clothes for the respect they seem to bring."

This story illustrates how people often judge others based on outward appearances rather than their true essence or inner wisdom. It challenges us to reconsider how we perceive and value others, emphasizing the importance of seeing beyond superficial appearances to recognize and appreciate someone's authentic self.

> *The human body is honoured to have the soul of humanity*
> *It is not beautiful clothes that are a sign of humanity.*
> *Persian poet and mystic Saadi*

Zarathustra and Yeshua taught people not to judge others based solely on their appearance. Yeshua often criticized the Pharisees for seeming religious on the outside while having different intentions inside. This lesson applies to ancient times and any religious or moral tradition today.

As Yeshua saw them, the Pharisees focused too much on following rules outwardly rather than living with true kindness and fairness inside. They cared more about looking good to others than genuinely being good people. Yeshua's teachings challenge all of us to look beyond appearances and seek inner growth and honesty instead. He encourages us to live authentically and genuinely, rather than just trying to impress others or follow rules for show.

There's a big difference between being conscious and being self-conscious. A conscious person lives with wisdom and awareness, focused on their inner values regardless of others' opinions. The Pharisees criticized Yeshua for not following certain religious rules, like who he ate with or worked with.

On the other hand, a self-conscious person worries too much about what others think. They don't live by their values but by trying to please others or avoid criticism. The term "Pharisee" also describes those who follow external rules without understanding their deeper meaning.

We shouldn't just see Pharisees as people from history or outside ourselves. We all have a Pharisee inside us—a part of us that acts unconsciously or out of fear. True righteousness comes from being conscious and wise, like the Magi or Wise Men, who live by inner understanding and integrity.

> *Beware of the teachers of the law. They like to walk around in flowing robes and love to be greeted with respect in the marketplaces and have the most important seats in the synagogues and the places of honor at banquets. They devour widows' houses and for a show make lengthy prayers. These men will be punished most severely.*[64]

Consciousness

In Zarathustra's teachings, consciousness and wisdom are regarded as the highest attributes of the Supreme Being (Ahura Mazda).[36] The relationship between Mazda and creation can be viewed as a seed within a tree. When the seed has grown into a tree, it becomes indistinguishable from the tree's essence. While traces of the seed can be found in the roots, trunk, branches, leaves, flowers, and fruit, the original seed has merged into the tree's core.

The tree simply couldn't exist without the seed. Even though it is no longer visible, the seed's presence continues to exist in every

---

[64] Luke 20:46-47

cell of the tree. Similarly, we can't directly see Ahura Mazda, as the seed has become invisible in the tree. The seed of Ahura Mazda's attributes manifests as wisdom and consciousness in our existence. We can only experience the Supreme Being within our consciousness and wisdom, as Zarathustra realized it.[65]

Yeshua, like Zarathustra, often told people to live a conscious life. In the Gospels, he says things like "Watch," "Be awake," and "Don't fall asleep." He talks about how problems happen when the master is absent, the farmer is sleeping, or the renters take over the vineyard.

> *And what I say to you I say to all: Stay awake.*[66]

For example, the night before his crucifixion, Yeshua asked his disciples to stay awake with him. These teachings show that Yeshua wanted people to be spiritually alert and mindful. He encouraged his followers to be aware of their actions and surroundings, ready to respond with wisdom and integrity to any challenges.

> *Then he returned to his disciples and found them sleeping. "Couldn't you men keep watch with me for one hour?" he asked Peter."*[67] *"Therefore keep watch, because you do not know on what day your Lord will come."*[68]

Yeshua often described unconscious people as "asleep." This metaphor is not about actual sleep, but about living life without awareness. He encouraged people to be conscious and aware in

---

[65] Yasna 45.8
[66] Mark 13:37
[67] Matthew 26:40
[68] Matthew 24:42

their lives. He often said, "Watch," which in Greek means "Be awake."

> *Therefore keep watch because you do not know when the owner of the house will come back—whether in the evening, or at midnight, or when the rooster crows, or at dawn.*[69]

Humans often get caught up in worldly things and forget to focus on their inner selves. We easily "fall asleep" in daily life and lose sight of our true purpose: to wake up and be conscious. Like Zarathustra, Yeshua teaches us about a higher level of existence, which he calls "The Awakening State" or "The Kingdom of Heaven."

It is hard to understand Yeshua's wisdom when we are in a state of unconsciousness. In our lower state of unconsciousness or sleepiness, we cannot grasp the true meaning of his messages. Even his own disciples were not always awake and could not fully understand his teachings. Yeshua said to Peter,

> *Get behind me, Satan! You are a stumbling block to me; you do not have in mind the concerns of God, but merely human concerns.*[70]

Many mistakes and errors occur in our lives when we are not aware and conscious. This is when, metaphorically, the weeds will grow among the wheat.

> *The kingdom of heaven is like a man who sowed good seed in his field. But while everyone was sleeping, his enemy came and sowed weeds among the wheat, and went away. When the wheat sprouted and formed heads, then the weeds also appeared.*[71]

---

[69] Mark 13:35

[70] Matthew 16:23

[71] Matthew 13:24-27

THE MESSIAH: SAOSHYANT

We cannot keep creating a mess and expect a savior to come and clean it for us. It's like sleeping all day, not working, not washing our dishes, and not paying our bills, then expecting someone to come and save us from our circumstances. We all have work to do to keep our minds pure and clear. We must elevate our consciousness and transform ourselves from water to wine, from a caterpillar to a butterfly. We must be conscious to embrace the light of wisdom like a lamp within, enabling us to see the awakened human beings and messiahs who come to guide us toward our higher selves (the Kingdom of Heaven). We have work to do before the guide arrives. It is the purpose of each man and woman to work on themselves, to listen to the wisdom of all those awakened humans, and to be conscious.[72]

Listen to the best words with attentive ears, and examine them with conscious thought and deep insight. Each man and woman should personally choose the path of good and avoid the path of bad (darkness).

Gathas: Yasna 30-2

There is a term in Zoroastrian tradition known as *Frashokereti*. It means "making wonderful / excellent." It is a notion of a final restoration of the universe to its original perfect creation. The Light will overcome darkness; Truth will win over lies and deception. The world will be reconstructed and governed by wisdom and consciousness again in perfect unity with the Supreme Being (Ahura Mazda).[73] *The world will be restored to its ideal condition.*[74]

---

[72] Yasna 46-10

[73] Yasna 30.8

[74] Yasna 30.9

According to the *Frashokereti* idea, humanity experiences a dark time in its lives. Ahriman (the Wicked Spirit) will dominate the Earth, spreading lies, deception, corruption, violence, and greed. However, there comes a time when humanity will wake up to its true nature of "goodness," "wisdom," and "consciousness."

With the guidance of Soashyants (guides, saviors), humanity will make the Earth like a paradise again. Humanity will regain "the golden age" of the original creation of peace and prosperity on Earth. Zarathustra was a *Soashyant*,[75] a savior of humanity to guide us toward healthier and more conscious life on Earth. He hoped that this restoration would occur by the end of his life.[76] However, he also pointed out that other Soashyantsand saviors would come after him to complete his mission and teachings on Earth.

However, since Zarathustra emphasizes everyone's responsibility for their thoughts, words, and actions, the coming of the Soshyants (messiah) does not mean that we should wait for them to come and save us from the corruption and chaos in the world. According to his teachings and the concept of Frashokereti, everyone is also responsible for bringing the world back to its original goodness. We all have an active duty towards the world's fate, working to make it a paradise again. Our task is to enhance our wisdom and awareness while safeguarding the Earth, all living creatures, and our existence.

In Eastern spirituality, there is a saying, "When the student is ready, the master will come." One does not know when the

---

[75] Yasna 50.11, Yasna 29.6-11

[76] Yasna 48.2, Yasna 34.15, Yasna 46.19

savior will arrive, but one needs to have enough willpower, determination, consciousness, and devotion to be awake for their coming.

"At that time the kingdom of heaven will be like ten virgins who took their lamps and went out to meet the bridegroom. 2 Five of them were foolish and five were wise. 3 The foolish ones took their lamps but did not take any oil with them. 4 The wise ones, however, took oil in jars along with their lamps. 5 The bridegroom was a long time in coming, and they all became drowsy and fell asleep.

6 "At midnight the cry rang out: 'Here's the bridegroom! Come out to meet him!'
7 "Then all the virgins woke up and trimmed their lamps.
8 The foolish ones said to the wise, 'Give us some of your oil; our lamps are going out.'
9 "'No,' they replied, 'there may not be enough for both us and you. Instead, go to those who sell oil and buy some for yourselves.'
10 "But while they were on their way to buy the oil, the bridegroom arrived. The virgins who were ready went in with him to the wedding banquet. And the door was shut.
11 "Later the others also came. 'Lord, Lord,' they said, 'open the door for us!'
12 "But he replied, 'Truly I tell you, I don't know you."
13 "Therefore keep watch, because you do not know the day or the hour."

Matthew 25:1-13

MAY THE SPIRIT OF LOVE AND WISDOM

OF MAZDA BE ALWAYS OUR GUIDE

www.zarathustra.ca

www.ingramcontent.com/pod-product-compliance
Lightning Source LLC
Chambersburg PA
CBHW070439010526
44118CB00014B/2114